On the farm

Illustrated by Luisa Laino

Houghton Mifflin Company • Boston
Atlanta • Dallas • Geneva, Illinois • Palo Alto • Princeton

I went to visit a farm one day

and saw a pig across the way.

Now what do you think

I heard it say?

Oink Oink Oink

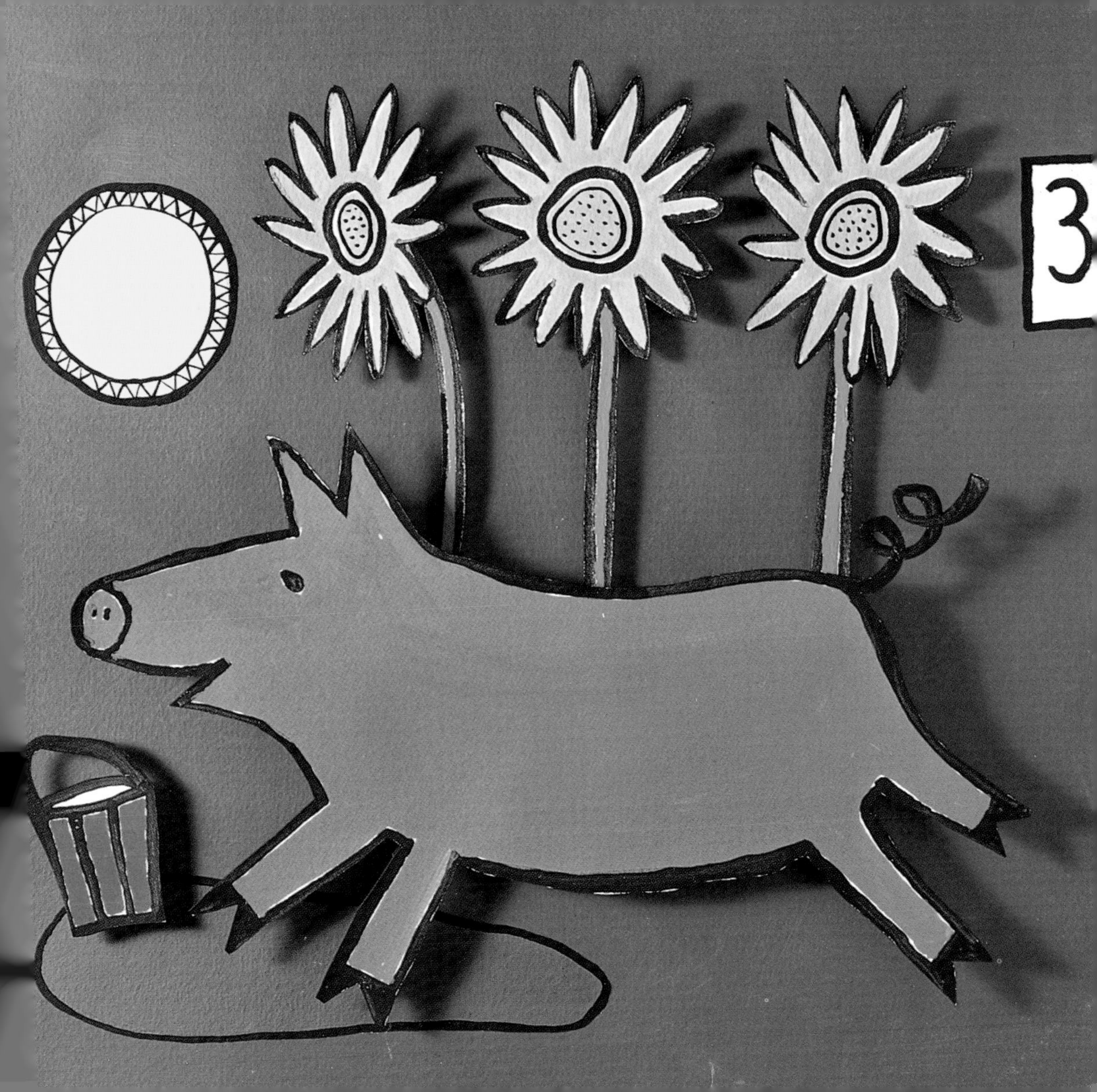
3

I went to visit a farm one day

and saw a sheep across the way.

Now what do you think

I heard it say?

Baa Baa Baa

I went to visit a farm one day

and saw a cow across the way.

Now what do you think

I heard it say?

6

Moo Moo Moo